T0198960

The Woodpile Kitty

Written by:

Diana Satkamp

Illustrated by:

Ed Gedeon

Copyright Page

AuthorHouse™
1663 Liberty Drive
Bloomington, IN 47403
www.authorhouse.com
Phone: 833-262-8899

This book is printed on acid-free paper.

ISBN: 978-1-4634-4386-3 (sc)

Print information available on the last page.

Published by AuthorHouse 03/02/2023

authorHOUSE®

Dedication

Thanks to Dr. Lynn Day and staff for all the wonderful care received by our animals over the years.

A special thank you to some of the present and past staff who adopted some of our kittens.

Hailey Newman

Matt Waggoner

Debbie Wease and Megan Wease

Jack and Diana were so excited to finally move into their new home.
The home had a long driveway leading up to the house.

Before they moved into their home, Diana said to Jack, "Please, no more cats." They already had three dogs. One was black and was named Lady, and the other two dogs were brown and white. Their names were Beauty and Whisk.

Well, it was not long before there was a black-and-brown cat hanging around in the woodpile behind the pole barn.

Jack fed her once, and then again. She would show up around the pile of wood for her morning and evening meals.

The winter came, and with it came snow!

The cat would still show up for a feeding once or twice a day. It was sometime in March, but not yet spring, and it was not as cold as winter. They noticed that the cat's tummy was growing.

When she walked, her tummy swung back and forth, and back and forth.

"Do you suppose that she is going to be having some kittens soon?"
said Jack to Diana.

The answer to his question took only a few days. She became the mother of four little kittens. Each kitten was a different color: one was black and white, one was blonde, one was many colors, and one was gray with black stripes. They were all so cute that you just wanted to pick them up and hold them in your hands.

Mama cat took very good care of the kittens by cleaning, feeding, and watching over them.

Mama cat did not want Jack and Diana to touch her kittens. In her own way, she was telling them to leave the kittens alone.

They decided to keep their distance so as to respect her and the kittens.

One day a kitten came leaping out of the woodpile, meowing loudly. It was as if the kitten were trying to say "Help me." The mama cat did not come and get the kitten.

Diana picked up the kitten and could see that her eyes were not open; they were matted together. She took some warm water and gently wiped the kitten's eyes.

Then she called Dr. Day's office and took the kitten to her animal hospital.

The doctor told them that the kitten had an eye infection. She gave them some medicine to put in the kitten's eyes. If they had not taken the kitten to the animal hospital, she could have lost her sight.

After they returned from the doctor, they could not put her back in the woodpile.

They decided to keep her in the house with their dogs.

They were so happy when the kitten's eyes seemed to get better almost overnight.

It took only a few days to think of a name for her, because she was black, white, and orange in color. They named her Patches.

Printed in the United States
by Baker & Taylor Publisher Services